REAL LIFE
MATH
ZOO
yet

**by Wendy Clemson, David Clemson,
and Ghislaine Sayers**

Ticktock

This library edition published in 2014 by Ticktock
First published in the USA in 2013 by Ticktock,
an imprint of Octopus Publishing Group Ltd

Distributed by Black Rabbit Books
P.O. Box 3263, Mankato, MN 56002

Copyright © Octopus Publishing Group Ltd 2014

With thanks to our consultants: Jenni Back and Liz Pumfrey from the NRICH Project,
Cambridge University, and Debra Voege.

Cataloging-in-Publication Data is available from the Library of Congress
ISBN 978 1 78325 197 1

Printed and bound in China

1 3 5 7 9 10 8 6 4 2

WENDY CLEMSON

Wendy is experienced in working with and for children, and has been writing full-time since 1989. Her publications, which now exceed one hundred, have been written for children and sometimes their parents and teachers. In her many math books, the aim is always to present the reader with challenges that are fun.

DAVID CLEMSON

David has wide-ranging experience as a writer and educationalist. His publications list is prodigious. In collaboration with Wendy, David has worked on many math books for children. He is fascinated by math and logic puzzles and is eager for the reader to enjoy them, too.

GHISLAINE SAYERS

Ghislaine began working with animals while still at school, helping on friends' farms and looking after her own pets. After graduating from high school, Ghislaine studied veterinary science at college and at London Zoo. Ghislaine has worked in a veterinary practice and with wild animals in Africa. She is now the zoo vet at Paignton Zoo in Devon, England.

CONTENTS

MATH SKILLS COVERED IN THIS BOOK:

CALCULATIONS:
Throughout this book there are opportunities to practice **addition**, **subtraction**, **multiplication**, and **division** using both mental calculation strategies and pencil and paper methods.

NUMBERS AND THE NUMBER SYSTEM:
- DECIMALS: pg. 8
- ESTIMATING (using a number line): pg. 27
- FRACTIONS: pgs. 8, 26
- NUMBER SEQUENCES: pg. 14
- ORDERING NUMBERS: pgs. 16, 27
- PERCENTAGES: pg. 12

SOLVING "REAL LIFE" PROBLEMS:
- MEASURES: pgs. 6, 8, 17, 18, 26
- MONEY: pgs. 24, 25
- TIME: pgs. 10, 11, 26

HANDLING DATA:
- BAR GRAPHS: pg. 22
- USING TABLES/CHARTS/DIAGRAMS: pgs. 6, 8, 10, 11, 12, 14, 16, 18, 21, 24, 27

MEASURES:
- AREA: pgs. 13, 21
- PERIMETER: pgs. 13, 20, 21
- RELATIONSHIPS BETWEEN UNITS OF MEASUREMENT: pg. 16
- SCALES (reading from scales): pg. 9
- USING MEASUREMENTS: pgs. 6, 8, 9, 13, 16, 17, 18, 20, 22, 26, 27
- VOCABULARY (time): pgs. 10, 11, 26, 27

SHAPE AND SPACE:
- 3-D SHAPES: pgs. 7, 13
- GRID COORDINATES: pg. 23

Supports math standards for ages 10+

HOW TO USE THIS BOOK

Math is important in the lives of people everywhere. We use math when we play a game, ride a bike, go shopping - in fact, all the time! Everyone needs to use math at work. You may not realize it, but a zoo vet uses math to care for an animal and even save its life! With this book you will get the chance to try lots of exciting math activities using real life animal data and facts about the work of zoo vets. Practice your math skills and experience the thrill of what it's really like to be a busy zoo vet.

This exciting math book is very easy to use – check out what's inside!

Fun-to-read information about animals and the work of zoo vets.

WORMING THE PRIMATES

All the animals at the zoo are wormed twice a year. Even if the fecal samples collected from an enclosure are negative, and do not show worm eggs, there may still be an animal in that enclosure with worms. The keepers might not have managed to collect feces from that animal. All the animals in an enclosure are given powdered anthelmintics (worming drugs) in a small amount of food, when they are hungry. The vets can then check how much of the drug has been eaten. The rest of the animals' food is given afterwards. If an animal's test is positive, showing it has worms, that animal is wormed more frequently.

MATH ACTIVITIES

Look for the
ZOO VET CASEBOOK.
You will find real life math activities and questions.

To answer some of the questions, you will need to collect data from a DATA BOX. Sometimes, you will need to collect facts and data from the text or from charts and diagrams.

Be prepared! You will need a pen or pencil and a notebook to figure out the answers.

ZOO VET CASEBOOK

Each of the **primates** at the zoo needs to eat a specific amount of worming drug for every pound of their body weight. To work out the correct amount of drug to give to each animal, the zoo vet needs to know how much each of the animals weighs.

In the DATA BOX you will see the weights of the primates at the zoo. Use the data to compare them.
1) Which primate is the heaviest?
2) Which primate is the lightest?
3) Name an animal that is heavier than an adult male ring-tailed lemur, but lighter than an adult female colobus monkey.
4) One of the primates and a crate weigh 6.5 lb. The crate weighs 5.5 lb. when empty. Which of the primates is it?

ANIMAL CARE FACT

Sometimes drugs are given in foods that the animals are not normally allowed to eat – a bit like a bribe! The colobus monkeys, spider monkeys, Diana monkeys, and swamp monkeys get their anthelmintic in mashed-banana sandwiches. The gorillas and orangutans have their worming drugs in a low-sugar blackcurrant drink.

ANIMAL CARE FACT

How do you weigh a gorilla? In the gorillas' den there is a special platform with scales underneath. Food is put on the platform and the scales are zeroed. A gorilla is let into the enclosure. The gorilla sits on the platform to eat the food and can be weighed while it is eating.

A zoo vet examines a ring-tailed lemur.

16

Fun-to-read zoo vet facts.

If you see one of these boxes, there will be important data inside that will help you with the math activities.

Feeling confident? Try these extra **CHALLENGE QUESTIONS.**

DATA BOX	PRIMATE WEIGHT CHART		
	PRIMATE	ADULT MALE	ADULT FEMALE
	Gorilla	308 lb.	176 lb.
	Orangutan	176 lb.	95 lb.
	Gibbon	14 lb.	14 lb.
	Ring-tailed lemur	8.5 lb.	7.5 lb.
	Howler monkey	20.5 lb.	20.5 lb.
	Golden lion tamarin	1 lb.	1 lb.
	Goeldi monkey	12 oz.	12 oz.
	Colobus monkey	27.5 lb.	19 lb.
	Spider monkey	24 lb.	24 lb.
	Diana monkey	21 lb.	21 lb.
	Swamp monkey	20 lb.	20 lb.

CHALLENGE QUESTION

See if you can answer this fun question. On one end of a seesaw there are five golden lion tamarins and a female colobus monkey.

Which of the primates could sit on the other end to balance the seesaw?

17

IF YOU NEED HELP...

TIPS FOR MATH SUCCESS

On pages 28–29 you will find lots of tips to help you with your math work.

ANSWERS

Turn to pages 30–31 to check your answers. (Try all the activities and questions before you take a look at the answers.)

GLOSSARY

On page 32 there is a glossary of zoo vet words and a glossary of math words. The glossary words appear **in bold** in the text.

ZOO VET TO THE RESCUE

Zoo vets work with wild animals from all over the world. Every day at work is different, and anything can happen! Your zoo has just received an emergency phone call from another zoo, hundreds of miles away. The other zoo has been flooded and their female giraffe, called Twizzle, urgently needs a new home. Your zoo has an enclosure for giraffes and a male giraffe who is waiting for a mate. You quickly agree that Twizzle can come to live at your zoo. First you will need to find a way to transport her. The zoo's truck is big enough to carry Twizzle, but she will need to be inside a smaller travelling crate. The crate will have to be built as quickly as possible.

ZOO VET CASEBOOK

The zoo's maintenance crew has sketched out some designs for the giraffe's crate. All of the crates are made from panels that are strong enough to withstand Twizzle's kicks. Now you need to think about all her other needs:

- Twizzle must be able to sit down, stand up, and turn around in her crate.
- The crate should have a roof made of netting or hessian (thick material).
- The crate must have ventilation (air holes). The ventilation holes must not allow Twizzle's horns to become stuck or be in a place where she can kick, as the crate will be weakened.
- The crate must be slightly taller than Twizzle.

Look at the six crate designs in the DATA BOX.

1) Which crate would you choose?
2) Why did you choose that crate? List your reasons.

(You will find a TIP to help you with these questions on page 28.)

Twizzle in the paddock at her old home

ANIMAL CARE FACT

The floor of the giraffe's crate must allow urine to drain away during the journey. A false floor is made for the crate from a metal grid. There will be a small gap between the grid and the bottom of the crate, which will allow any wetness to drain away, keeping Twizzle clean and dry. The walls of the crate and the grid on the floor will be padded with rubber matting to protect Twizzle during the journey. The floor must be comfortable to lie on, too, so the rubber matting will be covered in a thick layer of straw.

Body length: 11 feet

GIRAFFE CRATE DESIGNS

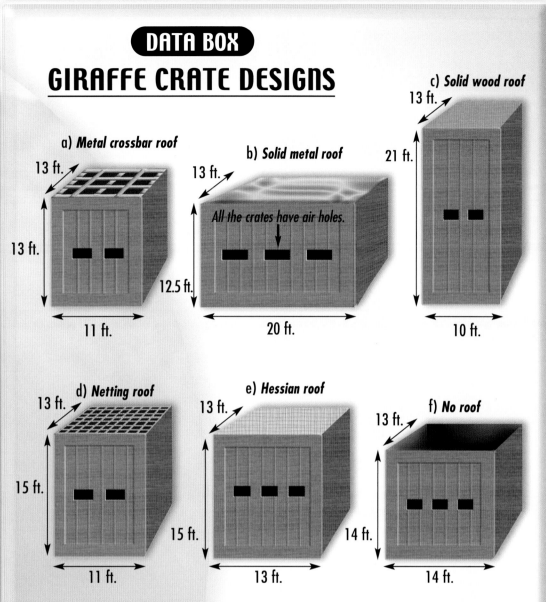

a) Metal crossbar roof
13 ft.
13 ft.
11 ft.

b) Solid metal roof
13 ft.
All the crates have air holes.
12.5 ft.
20 ft.

c) Solid wood roof
13 ft.
21 ft.
10 ft.

d) Netting roof
13 ft.
15 ft.
11 ft.

e) Hessian roof
13 ft.
15 ft.
13 ft.

f) No roof
13 ft.
14 ft.
14 ft.

Height: 14 feet

Weight: 2,000 pounds

CHALLENGE QUESTIONS

Here are some unusual crates that the zoo's maintenance crew is working on:

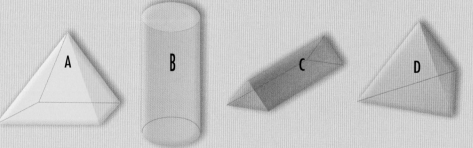

A   B   C   D

a) Match the name to the shape: cylinder, tetrahedron, square-based pyramid, triangular **prism**.
b) Which two shapes have five **faces**? Which of these has five **vertices**?
c) Which shape has the fewest faces?

SEDATING A GIRAFFE

You have arrived to pick up Twizzle from her old home, but first she will need to be given a **sedative** drug. The drug will make Twizzle feel calmer, and will ensure that she doesn't panic or hurt herself on the journey. Twizzle will be shut in her house and the sedative will be given by injection, using a dart shot from a dart gun. It is important that vets take their time and wait for exactly the right moment when darting an animal. If a vet misses with the first dart, an animal may panic. This makes it more difficult to get another shot. Before Twizzle can be darted, you will need to work out the correct amount of sedative to give her.

ZOO VET CASEBOOK

To work out the giraffe's drug dose you need to use **fractions** and **decimal fractions**.

1) Show what you know about how decimals and fractions are related by finding the missing numbers in this table:

?	1 ÷ 2	0.5
?	1 ÷ 4	?
?	?	0.75
¹⁄₁₀	?	?

2) What is one quarter of: 20, 80, 800?
3) What is one tenth of: 100, 50?

For every hundred pounds of her body weight, Twizzle needs 0.25 ounces of sedative drug.

4) If Twizzle weighs 2,000 lb., how many oz. of sedative should we give her?
5) In each fl. oz. of injection there is .50 oz. of drug. How many fl. oz. do you inject to sedate Twizzle?

The zookeeper reassures a sleepy Twizzle.

ANIMAL CARE FACT

The sedative dart will eventually fall out of Twizzle as she walks around her enclosure, and her keepers will then retrieve it. During Twizzle's journey, it will be the vet's job to make sure she is in the best possible health. Giraffes are big, but they are timid, and can easily be startled by loud noises. Twizzle must be handled gently at all times.

CHALLENGE QUESTION

Test your skill at reading measuring scales.

How much medicine is in each container?

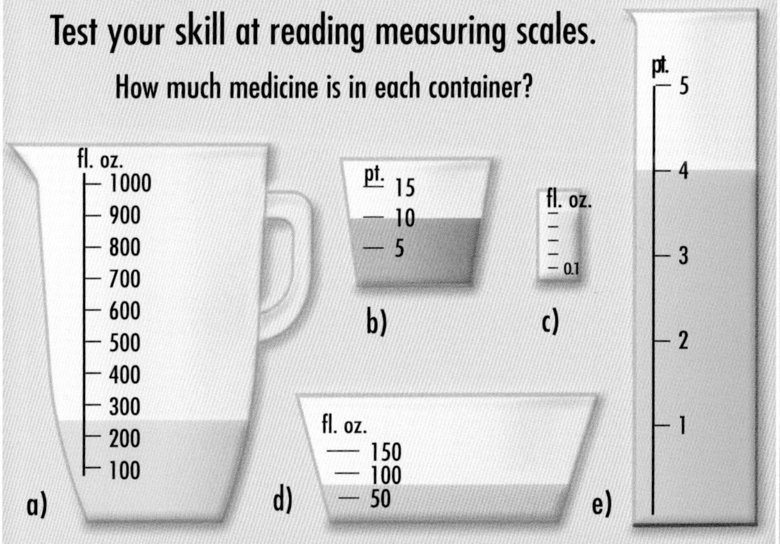

fl. oz.
- 1000
- 900
- 800
- 700
- 600
- 500
- 400
- 300
- 200
- 100

a)

pt. 15
- 10
- 5

b)

fl. oz.
- 0.1

c)

fl. oz.
- 150
- 100
- 50

d)

pt.
- 5
- 4
- 3
- 2
- 1

e)

(You will find information about UNITS OF MEASUREMENT on page 28.)

ANIMAL CARE FACT

When a giraffe is darted, it sometimes panics and runs. The vets and zookeepers have to make sure that the enclosure is safe before they dart Twizzle. They check that there are no sharp objects sticking out from the walls and remove the hay racks. The floor is covered in a deep layer of straw, so that it is not slippery.

TWIZZLE ON THE MOVE!

It takes 24 hours for the full effect of the **sedative** to work on Twizzle. The sedative will now keep her calm for approximately seven days. The next morning, when Twizzle is fully sedated, she is walked to the travelling crate. A pathway from the door of her enclosure to the back of the crate is walled with hessian to stop her seeing anything that may worry or scare her. The keepers gently coax Twizzle into the crate, tempting her with her favorite food – branches with leaves. When Twizzle is inside the crate, it is gently winched onto the truck. Twizzle is ready to go to her new home.

ZOO VET CASEBOOK

It is important to plan Twizzle's journey very carefully. She must be healthy and calm when she arrives at her new home.

- The truck will need to travel quite slowly, and so a short route must be chosen.
- The truck carrying Twizzle will be very tall, and so the route must avoid low bridges.
- Curvy roads must be avoided in case Twizzle topples over.
- Every three hours, the truck must stop at the side of the road for 30 minutes so that Twizzle can be checked and given some food and water.

In the DATA BOX you will see three possible routes.

Each black space on the routes represents 30 minutes (½ hour) of travelling time.

1) Which route will give you the fastest trip?

2) How long does the trip take?

(Don't forget that every three hours you need to add an extra 30 minutes for a checking and feeding stop. These are not shown on the route map.)

(You will find TIPS to help you with these questions on page 28.)

ANIMAL CARE FACT

The driver of the truck must be extremely careful when stopping, accelerating, and turning so Twizzle does not fall over. The driver must also choose quiet places to stop, so that Twizzle is not scared by noises and people while she has her food and water.

GIRAFFE FACT

Giraffes usually sleep standing up because it takes them a long time to get to their feet if they are approached by a predator. Although Twizzle is safe from predators in her enclosure at the zoo, her **instincts** still tell her to do this.

GIRAFFE FACTS

Giraffes are the tallest animals on Earth. They can run at speeds of up to 35 mph.

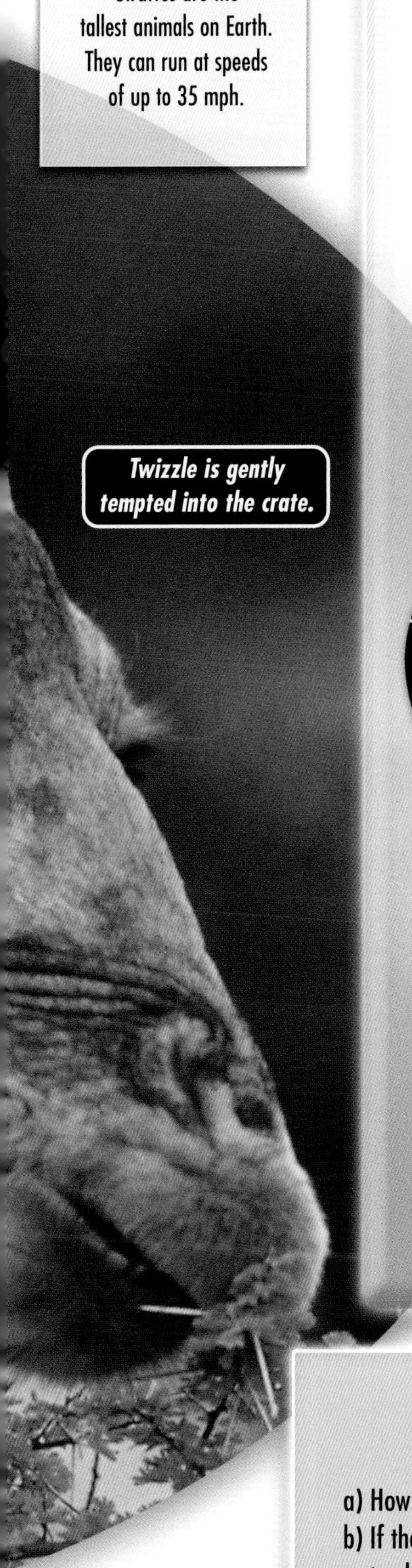

Twizzle is gently tempted into the crate.

DATA BOX TWIZZLE'S JOURNEY

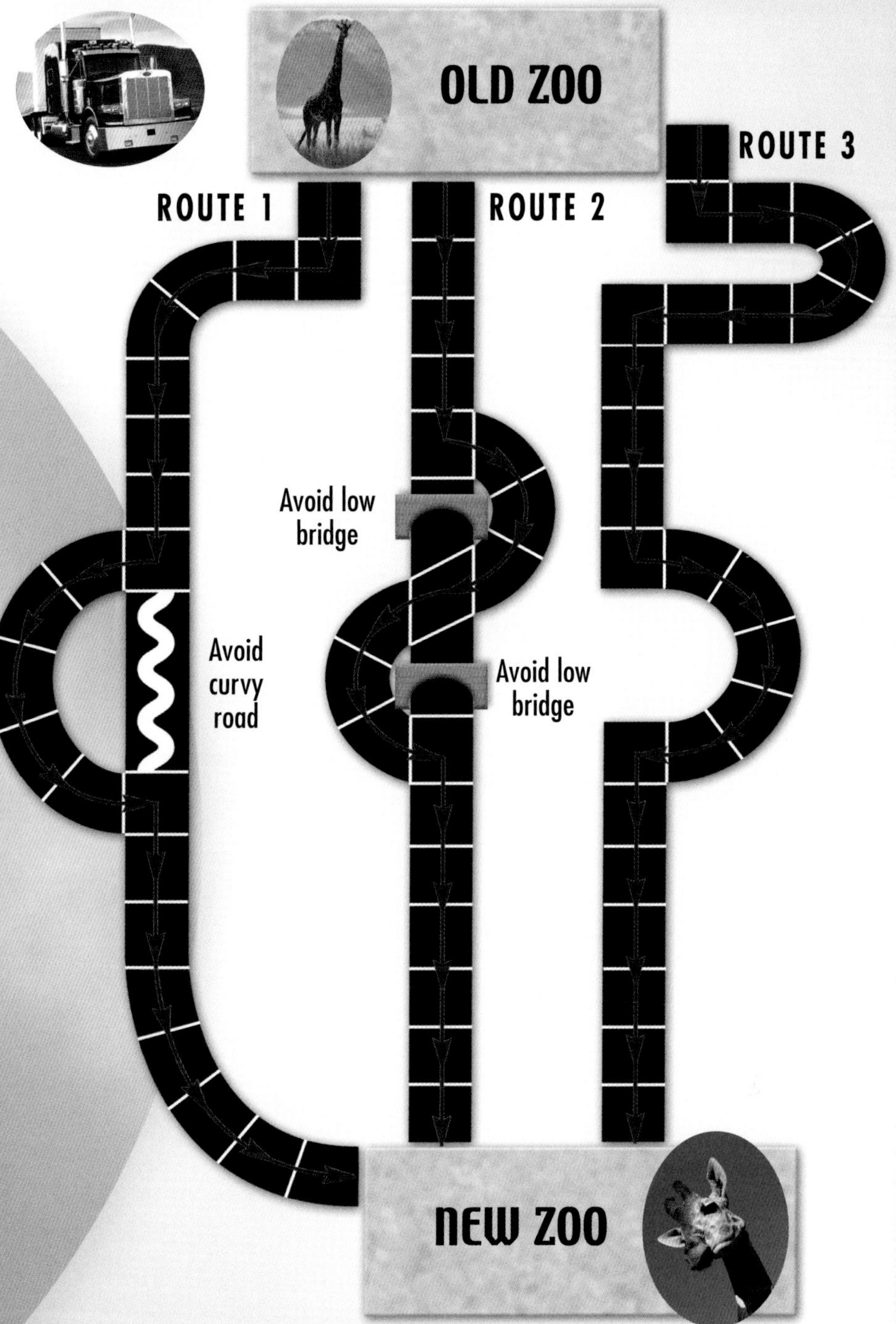

OLD ZOO
ROUTE 1
ROUTE 2
ROUTE 3
Avoid low bridge
Avoid curvy road
Avoid low bridge
NEW ZOO

CHALLENGE QUESTIONS

Use the routes in the DATA BOX to answer these questions:

a) How many checking and feeding stops would you have to make if you used ROUTE 3?

b) If the truck left the old zoo at 9:00 a.m. and took ROUTE 2, what time would it be when the truck stopped for Twizzle's second checkup?

c) Which route are you on if the total trip is 750 minutes (including the checking and feeding stops)?

(You will find TIPS to help you with these questions on page 28.)

A NEW HOME FOR TWIZZLE

When Twizzle arrives at her new home, she will need time to explore her surroundings and recover from the long journey. She will also want to find out which parts of her enclosure feel safe and where her food and water comes from. On arrival, Twizzle is coaxed from the crate and put inside the giraffe enclosure on her own. She can see and smell the male giraffe, but she will not be able to go near him for a few days. The keepers quietly watch over her, and give her lots of vegetables, fruit, and browse (branches with leaves). These foods contain a large amount of water. It is very important that Twizzle feeds and takes in enough fluids.

ZOO VET CASEBOOK

Zoo vets have to work out exactly how much food an animal needs for good health.

In the DATA BOX you will see a hundred square that shows a giraffe's diet. As you can see, the **fraction** $^{15}/_{100}$ is the part of the diet that is apples. This is 15 parts out of 100, or *15 percent*. The symbol for percent is %.

1) How much of the giraffe's diet is horse pellets?
2) What percentage is cabbage?
3) How much of the diet is apple and carrot added together?

(You will find help with using PERCENTAGES on page 28.)

ANIMAL CARE FACT

Sometimes animals will not eat in new surroundings. Powdered glucose and electrolytes (sugars and salts) are added to their drinking water to give them some energy.

Twizzle settles into her new home.

ZOO VET DIARY: TWIZZLE MEETS HER MATE

- A few days after her arrival at the zoo, Twizzle and the male giraffe were allowed together for a couple of hours, while the keepers kept watch.
- When the keepers were satisfied that the two giraffes were getting on well, Twizzle was able to stay with her new mate all the time, but only inside the giraffe house.
- After a few more days, Twizzle and the male were let out and allowed to stay together in the outside enclosure.

DATA BOX GIRAFFE DIET

🐾 **Horse pellets**	✗ **Carrots**	
🦴 **Browse concentrate**	✿ **Cabbages**	
🍎 **Apples**	🌿 **Browse (branches)**	

CHALLENGE QUESTIONS

The keepers have been busy collecting straw bales to build Twizzle a comfortable bed. They use a small electric vehicle called a *gator* to drive around the zoo.

a) The gator is partly full of straw bales. How many more bales will fill the gator? Is it 16, 18, 8, or 14?

The straw bales are 2 yards long and 1 yard wide. Twizzle's bed needs to be 8 yards long and 6 yards wide.

b) How many bales are needed to build the bed?

c) If the bed only needs to be half a bale deep, the bales can be sliced in two. How many bales are needed then?

13

CHECKING FOR PARASITES

It is spring – time to test all the animals at the zoo for worms! **Parasitic** worms can harm the animals and cause diarrhea and weight loss. The parasitic worms lay their eggs in the animals' guts, then the eggs are passed out in the animals' feces (droppings). The eggs lie on the ground, and when the animals eat the grass or plants in their enclosures, they sometimes also eat the worm eggs. The eggs then go back into the animals' stomachs and develop into more worms. All zoo animals need to be checked twice a year to make sure that the number of parasites doesn't build up inside them, making them ill.

ZOO VET CASEBOOK

Wearing gloves, the vets and keepers collect feces from all the enclosures at the zoo, and then they test the feces to check for worms. The number of worms in an animal's stomach depends on how quickly new worms are born.

If the number of worms doubled every 4 weeks, we could make a table like this:

WEEKS	0	1	2	3	4	5	6	7	8	9	10	11	12
Number of worms if the number doubles every 4 weeks	1 WORM				2 WORMS				4 WORMS				8 WORMS

Can you see how this works? Now try to complete this table.

WEEKS	0	1	2	3	4	5	6	7	8	9	10	11	12
Number of worms if the number doubles every 3 weeks	1 WORM			2 WORMS			?			?			?
Every 2 weeks	1 WORM		2 WORMS		?		?		16 WORMS		?		?
Every week	1 WORM	2 WORMS	?	?	?	?	?	?	?	?	?	?	?

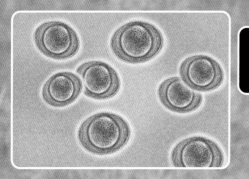

Toxocara worm eggs (from a cheetah) viewed through a microscope

(You will find a TIP to help you with this question on page 28.)

ZOO VET DIARY:
FECES COLLECTION WEEK!

- Some enclosures at the zoo have a whole family of animals living there. A small amount of feces has to be collected from lots of different piles. Hopefully there will be some from each animal.

- Some worms don't lay eggs every day, and so feces is collected for three consecutive days.

- In the zoo lab, each of the feces samples is tested. Water and a small amount of feces from each sample is shaken up with glass beads, which breaks up the feces.

- The liquid feces is then sieved. The microscopic worm eggs and water pass through the sieve and into a test tube.

- The test tube then goes into a centrifuge. This machine spins the tube and liquid very quickly and forces all the eggs to the bottom of the tube. The water is then poured away.

- A special solution is added to make the eggs float. The eggs are then collected with a pipette, put on a glass slide, and counted under a microscope.

CHALLENGE QUESTION
Cheetahs can have a parasitic worm called toxocara. A female toxocara worm can lay 700 eggs in each ounce of cheetah feces.

If a cheetah produces 30 ounces of feces in a day, and has one toxocara worm in its stomach, how many worm eggs will have been laid?

ANIMAL CARE FACT
Animals in zoos need to be wormed because they live in the same enclosures all the time and may eat grass or food contaminated by worm eggs. In the wild, animals move from place to place, and so there is less chance of them eating worm eggs.

WORMING THE PRIMATES

All the animals at the zoo are wormed twice a year. Even if the fecal samples collected from an enclosure are negative, and do not show worm eggs, there may still be an animal in that enclosure with worms. The keepers might not have managed to collect feces from that animal. All the animals in an enclosure are given powdered anthelmintics (worming drugs) in a small amount of food, when they are hungry. The vets can then check how much of the drug has been eaten. The rest of the animals' food is given afterwards. If an animal's test is positive, showing it has worms, that animal is wormed more frequently.

ZOO VET CASEBOOK

Each of the **primates** at the zoo needs to eat a specific amount of worming drug for every pound of its body weight. To work out the correct amount of drug to give to each animal, the zoo vet needs to know how much each of the animals weighs.

In the DATA BOX you will see the weights of the primates at the zoo.
Use the data to compare them.

1) Which primate is the heaviest?
2) Which primate is the lightest?
3) Name an animal that is heavier than an adult male ring-tailed lemur, but lighter than an adult female colobus monkey.
4) One of the primates and a crate weigh 6.5 lb. The crate weighs 5.5 lb. when empty. Which of the primates is it?

(You will find a TIP to help you with these questions on page 28.)

ANIMAL CARE FACT

Sometimes drugs are given in foods that the animals are not normally allowed to eat — a bit like a bribe! The colobus monkeys, spider monkeys, Diana monkeys, and swamp monkeys get their anthelmintic in mashed-banana sandwiches. The gorillas and orangutans have their worming drugs in a low-sugar blackcurrant drink.

ANIMAL CARE FACT

How do you weigh a gorilla?
In the gorillas' den there is a special platform with scales underneath. Food is put on the platform and the scales are zeroed. A gorilla is let into the enclosure. The gorilla sits on the platform to eat the food and can be weighed while it is eating.

A zoo vet examines a ring-tailed lemur.

DATA BOX PRIMATE WEIGHT CHART

PRIMATE	ADULT MALE	ADULT FEMALE
Gorilla	308 lb.	176 lb.
Orangutan	176 lb.	95 lb.
Gibbon	14 lb.	14 lb.
Ring-tailed lemur	8.5 lb.	7.5 lb.
Howler monkey	20.5 lb.	20.5 lb.
Golden lion tamarin	1 lb.	1 lb.
Goeldi monkey	12 oz.	12 oz.
Colobus monkey	27.5 lb.	19 lb.
Spider monkey	24 lb.	24 lb.
Diana monkey	21 lb.	21 lb.
Swamp monkey	20 lb.	20 lb.

CHALLENGE QUESTION

See if you can answer this fun question. On one end of a seesaw there are five golden lion tamarins and a female colobus monkey.

Which of the primates could sit on the other end to balance the seesaw?

MEDICAL EMERGENCY: POISONING

You have just received an urgent text message. One of the wolves is ill. He has collapsed, is having fits, and is hardly breathing. When you get to "Wolf Wood," you see there is vomit in the enclosure. Wearing gloves, you examine the vomit to see if you can find a clue as to why the wolf is ill. The vomit smells very sweet and you find pieces of foil and a substance that looks suspiciously like chocolate. Someone has thrown their candy into the wolves' enclosure. Many animals, including *canids* (the dog family), can be poisoned by chocolate. There is no cure — all a vet can do is support the animal while it tries to recover.

ZOO VET CASEBOOK

The wolf is placed in a large crate and rushed to the treatment room in the zoo hospital.

A catheter (thin tube) is put into a vein in one of the wolf's front legs. The catheter is used to give drugs and fluids and to take blood samples for testing. The wolf needs to be given fluids to maintain his blood pressure and stop him from going into shock.

1) Every hour the wolf is given 0.5 oz. of fluids for every pound that he weighs. If the wolf weighs 60 lb., how many oz. of fluids is he given each hour?
2) How many oz. of fluids will the wolf be given in 5 minutes?
3) If there are 20 drops of fluid in 1 oz., how many drops is the wolf given in 5 minutes?

> Wolf bites can be serious, and so the wolf is given anesthetic gas mixed with oxygen to keep him calm while he is being treated.

CHALLENGE QUESTIONS

Many animals have a specialized diet and can become very ill or overweight if they eat the wrong foods. Sometimes they can even die.

Study the food chart in the DATA BOX.

Which of the animals should eat: a) Grass b) Bread c) Chicken
Which of the animals must not eat: d) Chocolate e) Meat f) Boxwood g) Ragwort
h) For which of the animals might these food bowls be prepared?

Food bowl A

Food bowl B

Food bowl C

FOOD CHART

NAME OF ANIMAL	FOODS FOR GOOD HEALTH							POISONOUS FOODS			
	GRASS	MAIZE	BREAD	CHICKEN	MEAT ON THE BONE	STRAW	VEGETABLES	MEAT	CHOCOLATE	BOXWOOD (PLANT)	RAGWORT (PLANT)
ELEPHANT		✔	✔			✔	✔	✔			
ASIATIC LION				✔	✔				✔		
ZEBRA	✔						✔			✔	
KANGAROO	✔		✔				✔				✔
WOLF				✔	✔				✔		

ZOO VET DIARY: SAVING THE WOLF

- When the wolf arrived in the zoo hospital, he was given oxygen (by mask) and his heart rate and rhythm were checked with a stethoscope. His temperature, respiration rate (breathing), and blood pressure were monitored at all times.

- Blood samples were sent straight to the lab for analysis. The wolf was given a drug to sedate him slightly and decrease the spasms. Then he was given fluids.

- After four hours, the wolf started to improve, and he was moved to the recovery pens. During the night, the wolf was checked every three hours to make sure the spasms hadn't started again.

- The next day, the wolf was given a small amount of high-energy, easy-to-digest food. His medication was hidden in the food. A week later, the wolf was well enough to go back to his family.

ANIMAL CARE FACT

Visitors to zoos often throw their own food into the animals' enclosures. Sometimes visitors pick leaves from bushes growing outside the enclosure and throw these in, not knowing whether they are poisonous or not. Notices at zoos asking visitors not to feed the animals SHOULD NEVER BE IGNORED.

One of the vets prepares to treat the wolf.

THE RED RIVER HOGS MOVE IN

In a couple of weeks there will be some more new arrivals. Preparations are underway to welcome three red river hogs that are moving from another zoo. Red river hogs are found in Africa and Madagascar, where they live wild in forests and warm, moist woodlands. Red river hogs spend a lot of time rooting in the soil with their noses, looking for food. They can soon turn a wooded area into a muddy field. The keepers have chosen a space for the hogs' enclosure where there is thick undergrowth and lots of trees. Now you need to help plan their new home.

ZOO VET CASEBOOK

There are lots of important safety precautions to remember when planning a zoo enclosure.

- The fence around the enclosure will go under the soil for 20 inches to prevent the hogs from digging out.
- The fence will be 5 feet high, to stop visitors leaning over.
- Around the edge of the enclosure there will be a *stand off* barrier. This extra barrier is 3 feet from the main fence, and it stops visitors from putting their fingers through the main fence where they could receive a bite from a hog!

The hogs' enclosure will be a rectangle, 320 feet long and 140 feet wide.

1) What is the enclosure's **perimeter**?
2) If each fence panel is 4 feet wide, how many panels are needed?

(You will find a TIP to help you with question 1 on page 28.)

ANIMAL CARE FACT

When the red river hogs arrive at the zoo, they will go into their new enclosure over a weighbridge. The vet and keepers will then know how much each hog weighs. This information will be useful if the vet needs to give the hogs medication, or if the females become pregnant.

RED RIVER HOG FACT

Red river hogs are inquisitive, intelligent, and quite strong. They can weigh up to 265 pounds. The hogs' sense of smell and hearing are very good and they communicate with each other constantly, using squeaks, chirps, and grunts.

ANIMAL CARE FACT

The red river hogs will have a house in their enclosure to give them shelter. Half of the house will have a glass window, so that visitors can see the hogs when they are inside. The other half of the house is closed in. This gives the hogs a quiet area away from visitors and a private place to give birth.

CHALLENGE QUESTIONS

Zoos want their animals to have as much space as possible, and their visitors to have a good view of the animals.

When planning an enclosure, the longer the perimeter fence, the better. Here are some drawings of zoo enclosures.

A B C D

a) What do you notice about the size of the space inside each enclosure?

b) Which of the enclosures has the longest perimeter fence?

(You will find a TIP to help you with question b on page 29.)

AMELIA'S DIET

The red river hogs have settled into their new home. However, one of the hogs, Amelia, is losing weight. There could be lots of reasons why Amelia is getting thinner. She may have a sore mouth or a bad tooth, the keepers may not be feeding the hogs enough, or Amelia might have worms. You talk through the problem with the hogs' keeper, but there are no clues. When you visit the hogs' enclosure at feeding time, you notice that the two fatter pigs keep chasing Amelia away from the food. Although Amelia is thin, she doesn't seem ill and is still bright, alert, and active. You decide Amelia will be given more food and her weight will be monitored.

ZOO VET CASEBOOK

Each day at feeding time, Amelia is shut in the house to eat on her own. She is also given extra food. Some scales are put in the hogs' house, and sometimes Amelia is given her food while she's on the scales, so that her weight can be checked while she is busy eating.

Now Amelia has enough food all to herself, she starts to steadily gain weight. This *bar graph* shows Amelia's weight over several weeks.

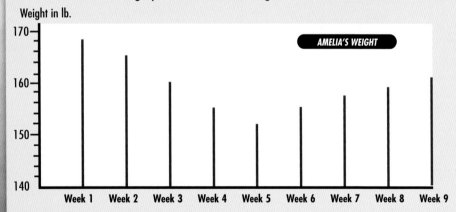

Amelia's healthy weight is shown in week 1.

1) What is Amelia's healthy weight?

2) For how many weeks does Amelia lose weight?

3) How much weight does Amelia gain from week 5 to week 6?

4) In weeks 7, 8, and 9, Amelia gains weight at a steady rate. How do we know this?

5) If Amelia goes on gaining weight at a steady rate, how many more weeks will it take to nearly reach her healthy weight?

(You will find information about BAR GRAPHS on page 29.)

RED RIVER HOG FACT

In the wild, red river hogs feed on a wide range of plant material, such as fungi, ferns, grasses, leaves, roots, bulbs, and fruits. They also eat insect larvae, frogs, mice, and earthworms. In the zoo, the hogs eat apples, bananas, carrots, cabbage, lettuce, bread, and tomatoes. They are also given vitamins, pelleted food, and chicks, for protein.

ANIMAL CARE FACT

When the hogs first moved into their new home they were getting a huge amount of food by eating the plants in their enclosure. Now the plants have all been eaten, the hogs' food will be increased by 50%. The food is also spread around the whole enclosure so that each hog has a chance to find food without being bullied by the others. Searching for food also gives the hogs more to do during the day.

CHALLENGE QUESTION

The edge of this grid is the fence around the hogs' enclosure. Food has been placed at (1, 2) and (3, 1).

Food is not placed along the fence. At what other coordinates can food be placed?

(You will find a TIP to help you with this question on page 29.)

MONEY MATTERS

Many species of wild animals are **endangered** because humans are hunting them illegally or destroying their natural habitats. Lots of zoos around the world are now involved with important **conservation** and **research** work. These zoos give endangered animals a safe place to live. The zoos also run **breeding programs** and they study the animals to find ways to help them in the wild. However, it costs hundreds of thousands of dollars each year to run a zoo, with lots of bills to be paid – food, medical care, heating, and wages. Zoos raise the funds to pay for their work in many different ways – donations, entrance fees, animal adoptions, and gift shops.

ZOO VET CASEBOOK

Zoo shops sell lots of fun gifts to their visitors. The profits the zoos make in their gift shops help to pay for the care of the animals.

Use the gift shop price list in the DATA BOX to help you answer these money questions.

1) What is the total cost of an orangutan T-shirt and a zebra soft toy?
2) A visitor pays for a giraffe soft toy with two $1 coins and two quarters. How much change does she get?
3) If you buy a lion baseball cap, what change will you get from a $10 note?
4) How many postcards can be bought for $1.60?
5) Which of these can be bought for less than $9?
   • A pencil case and a set of three ballpoint pens.
   • A gorilla soft toy and a zebra soft toy.
   • A notebook and a flamingo soft toy.
6) A visitor puts these coins into the zoo fund collecting box: 8 nickels, 2 dimes, 3 quarters, 11 cents.
   How much is that altogether?

(You will find TIPS to help you with these questions on page 29.)

SAVE THE
ORANGUTANS

CONSERVATION WORK FACT

Zoo vets make sure that animals living in zoos are kept in the best possible conditions. When animals are happy and healthy, they are more likely to breed. If animals breed well, their numbers will increase. Sometimes this means endangered animals can be reintroduced to the wild, to live in protected areas.

DATA BOX GIFT SHOP PRICE LIST

Ballpoint pens (set of three)	$ 3.00
Flamingo soft toy	$ 7.99
Giraffe soft toy	$ 2.30
Orangutan T-shirt	$10.95
Lion baseball cap	$ 3.95
Notebook	$ 3.75
Gorilla soft toy	$ 4.00
Pencil case	$ 3.50
Postcard	20¢
Zebra soft toy	$ 4.99

This baby orangutan was born in the zoo. Orangutans are critically endangered. There are fewer than 25,000 left in the world!

A baby African elephant born at the zoo

CHALLENGE QUESTIONS

Many zoos run adoption programs where you can pay a sum of money to adopt an animal. You don't get to take the animal home, but your money will help to pay for the animal's food and medical care.

Here are some adoption rates at the zoo:
• $1.50 a year for a llama.
• $2.75 a year for a hippopotamus.
• $5.25 a year for an elephant.

a) If you had $5, for how long could you adopt a llama?
b) If you had $5, for how long could you adopt a hippopotamus?
c) If you had $20, which animals could you adopt and for how long?

TWIZZLE HAS A BABY!

Nearly two years have passed since Twizzle arrived at the zoo, and this morning she has given birth to a calf. However, from the moment the calf was born, Twizzle has ignored her baby, and her keepers are now very worried. The calf is taking his first faltering steps, but he isn't suckling and Twizzle is starting to become aggressive towards him. It is decided that the calf will be taken from Twizzle for his own safety. A mother's milk and **colostrum** are the best food for a newborn animal, but Twizzle is a first-time mom, and she doesn't seem to know what to do. Hopefully next time Twizzle has a baby, she will be a better mom.

ZOO VET CASEBOOK

Twizzle is let out of the calving pen and the keepers catch the calf to feed him. For the first few days, the baby will need to be fed colostrum, from a bottle, six times a day. After a few days, the colostrum will be replaced by milk.

On day 1, the calf has six feeds starting at 6:00 a.m. and finishing at 9:00 p.m.

1) If the feeds are evenly spaced throughout the day, at what times is the calf fed?

On day 1, the calf weighs 120 lb.

2) The calf is fed one tenth of his weight. How much is that?

3) How much food is the calf given at each feeding?

4) If the calf only eats half of the food each time, how much food does he eat at each feeding?

5) Next day, the calf eats three-quarters of the food each time he is fed. How much food is that at each feeding?

ANIMAL CARE FACT

Giraffes have a **gestation period** of 15 to 16 months. Elephants have the longest gestation period of any mammal, about 22 months – that's nearly two years!

Bottle-feeding the calf

Twizzle's calf is nearly 7 feet tall when he is born.

ZOO VET DIARY: TWIZZLE'S CALF

- When Twizzle was about to give birth, her udders started to produce milk and swell up.
- Twizzle was separated from her mate, and video cameras were set up in the enclosure so that her keepers could watch her without disturbing her.
- One morning, Twizzle began pacing up and down and she was not interested in her food. Later that day she gave birth.
- Like most giraffes, Twizzle gave birth standing up and her calf dropped onto the straw on the floor of the enclosure. However, Twizzle was completely disinterested in her calf and walked away.
- The keepers are now hand-rearing Twizzle's baby. After each feed, the keepers have to make the calf urinate and pass feces by wiping his rear end with a damp cloth. Normally his mother would do this with her tongue.

DATA BOX ZOO BABIES

ANIMAL	GESTATION PERIOD	WEIGHT AT BIRTH
GIRAFFE	15 months	120 lb.
RED RIVER HOG	120-127 days	1.5 lb.
PANDA	45 days	3.5 oz.
RING-TAILED LEMUR	134 days	1.5 oz.
ELEPHANT	22 months	200 lb.
GORILLA	8.5 months	70.5 oz.
LION	14-15 weeks	3 lb.
MOUSE	21 days	0.05 oz.
GIANT ANTEATER	190 days	2.50 lb.
MALAYAN TAPIR	13 months	22 lb.
GRAY WOLF	63 days	1 lb.
MOUNTAIN ZEBRA	12 months	55 lb.

CHALLENGE QUESTIONS

Zoo vets need to be able to figure out when animals will have their babies.

a) It is March and five animals at the zoo have become pregnant. The timeline shows when the five babies will be born. Figure out what type of animal each of the babies is by using the information about gestation periods in the DATA BOX.

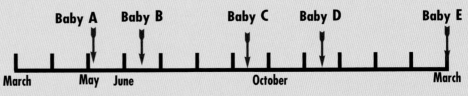

b) Put all the animals in the DATA BOX in order of their birth weight, starting with the heaviest.

(You will find TIPS to help you with these questions on page 29.)

TIPS FOR MATH SUCCESS

PAGES 6–7

ZOO VET CASEBOOK

Handling data:

TIP: You need to ask these questions about each crate:

- Is the crate tall enough?
- All of the crates are 13 feet deep, but is the crate wide enough for the length of Twizzle's body?
- What is the roof made of?

PAGES 8–9

Units of measurement:

There are two systems of measurement. The customary system uses inches, feet, miles, ounces, and pounds. The metric system uses centimeters, meters, kilometers, grams, and kilograms.

METRIC		CUSTOMARY	
Length		**Length**	
1 millimeter (mm)		1 inch (in.)	
1 centimeter (cm)	= 10 mm	1 foot (ft.)	= 12 in.
1 meter (m)	= 100 cm	1 yard (yd.)	= 3 ft.
1 kilometer (km)	= 1,000 m	1 mile	= 1,760 yd.
Weight		**Weight**	
1 gram (g)		1 ounce (oz.)	
1 kilogram (kg)	= 1,000 g	1 pound (lb.)	= 16 oz.
Capacity		**Capacity**	
1 milliliter (ml)		1 fluid ounce (fl. oz.)	
1 centiliter (cl)	= 10 ml	1 pint (pt.)	= 16 fl. oz.
1 liter (l)	= 1,000 ml		

Comparing metric and customary measurements:

1 kilometer = 0.62 of a mile
1 kilogram = 2.2 pounds
0.47 liter = 1 pint

PAGES 10–11

ZOO VET CASEBOOK

TIP: There are many good ways to work out how long the trips will take. One method is to count the spaces on each route in twos (two spaces = 1 hour travelling time). Then divide that total by three to give the number of half-hour breaks to add. Remember, there are 60 minutes in one hour.

PAGES 12–13

ZOO VET CASEBOOK

Using percentages:

Percent is a special form of a **fraction** and means *"part of 100."* For example: 50% is $^{50}/_{100}$ and 25% is $^{25}/_{100}$. Percentages are very useful for comparing amounts. They are often used in shops when prices are lowered in a sale. If an item costs $1.00 you might see: 50% OFF — this means the item now costs 50¢.

PAGES 14–15

CHALLENGE QUESTION

Multiplication:

When multiplying hundreds, for example 200 x 300, try this method: multiply 2 x 3 to get 6, and then look at the total number of zeros in 200 and 300. There are four zeros, so your answer is 60,000.
Check your answer with: 2 x 300 = 600
20 x 300 = 6,000   200 x 300 = 60,000

PAGES 16–17

ZOO VET CASEBOOK

Using units of measurement:

TIP: When you are given measurements in mixed units, it can be helpful to convert them all to the same unit so that they can be compared or used in calculations.

For example, 6.5 lb. and 8 oz. can be compared as 104 oz. and 8 oz. or as 6.5 lb. and 0.5 lb.

PAGES 20–21

ZOO VET CASEBOOK

Measuring perimeter:

TIP: With rectangles you can find the **perimeter** in three different ways:

- Add all four sides.
- Add one long and one short side and then double the answer.
- Double the length of the long side, double the length of the short side, and add the totals together.

5 ft.

3 ft.   3 ft.

5 ft.

For example, the perimeter of this rectangle is 16 ft.

PAGES 20–21 continued

CHALLENGE QUESTION

Measuring perimeter and area:

TIP: To find the **perimeter** of the enclosures, you can count the outer edges of the squares along the outside of each shape. We call the space inside the shapes the **AREA**.

PAGES 22–23

ZOO VET CASEBOOK

Interpreting a bar graph:

The graph on page 22 is known as a *bar graph*. In this case we could connect the tops of the lines to make a continuous bar graph. The left-hand side does not start at 0 lb. for two reasons: a hog will never weigh 0 lb., and starting at 140 lb. makes the graph clearer.

CHALLENGE QUESTION

Using coordinates:

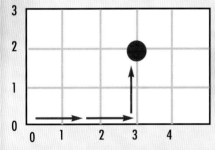

To find the coordinates of a point on a grid, you read along the bottom of the grid first and then up the side of the grid.

For example, a grid reference of **(3,2)** means **3 steps** along the bottom and then **2 steps** up to find the exact spot.

PAGES 24–25

ZOO VET CASEBOOK

Solving word problems involving money:

When doing shopping calculations, you can round up prices to find approximate amounts. So $3.99 can be rounded to $4 to make mental work easier. Don't forget to take away 1¢ off the $4 to get the answer at the end!

Counting up helps us to calculate our change:
If an item costs $4.95, and we pay with a $10 note, we can say, *"four dollars ninety-five cents plus five cents equals five dollars"* and *"five dollars plus five dollars equals ten dollars,"* and so the change is *"five cents plus five dollars,"* which is $5.05.

PAGES 26–27

CHALLENGE QUESTIONS

Measuring time using a number line:

A timeline is a kind of number line. Number lines are continuous and reach forever in both directions. We can make number lines to help in understanding and working with numbers.

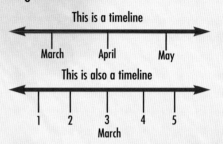

TIP: When you are given periods of time or measurements in mixed units, it can be helpful to convert them all to the same unit so that they can be compared. There are:

- 7 days in one week.
- 4 to 5 weeks in one month.
- 12 months or 52 weeks in one year.

(You can use a calendar to find out the exact number of days in each month.)

ANSWERS ANSWERS ANSWERS

PAGES 6–7

ZOO VET CASEBOOK

1) Crate e
2) Crate e is the most suitable for Twizzle because:
   • The crate is taller than Twizzle, but not too tall.
   • The crate is big enough that Twizzle has room to turn around (her body is 11 feet long).
   • The crate has a hessian roof.

CHALLENGE QUESTIONS

a) The names of the shapes are:

A: Square-based pyramid   B: Cylinder

C: Triangular prism   D: Tetrahedron

b) The square-based pyramid and triangular **prism** have five **faces**. The square based pyramid has five **vertices**.
c) The cylinder has the fewest faces. It has two circular faces and a curved surface along the length.

PAGES 8–9

ZOO VET CASEBOOK

1) The completed table should look like this:

½	1 ÷ 2	0.5
¼	1 ÷ 4	0.25
¾	3 ÷ 4	0.75
¹⁄₁₀	1 ÷ 10	0.1

2) One quarter of 20 is 5, 80 is 20, 800 is 200.
3) One tenth of 100 is 10, one tenth of 50 is 5.
4) Twizzle should be given 5 fl. oz. of drug.
5) We need to inject 10 fl. oz. to sedate Twizzle.

PAGES 8–9 continued

CHALLENGE QUESTION

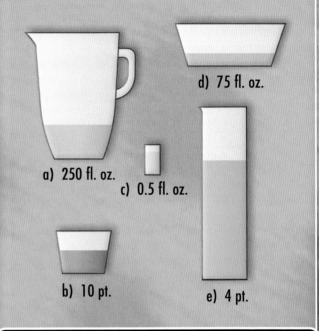

a) 250 fl. oz.
b) 10 pt.
c) 0.5 fl. oz.
d) 75 fl. oz.
e) 4 pt.

PAGES 10–11

ZOO VET CASEBOOK

1) Route 2 gives the fastest journey time.
2) It will take 11 hours to reach the new zoo (9.5 hours travelling and three stops of 30 minutes each).

CHALLENGE QUESTIONS

a) You would make 4 checking and feeding stops.
b) Twizzle's second check-up would start at 3:30 p.m.
c) Route 1

PAGES 12–13

ZOO VET CASEBOOK

1) 20% (or ⅕) of the diet is horse pellets.
2) 10% (or ¹⁄₁₀) of the diet is cabbage.
3) 30% of the diet is apple and carrot added together.

CHALLENGE QUESTIONS

a) 14 more bales will fill the gator.
b) 24 bales are needed to build Twizzle's bed.
c) 12 bales are needed if they are sliced in two.

ANSWERS

PAGES 14–15

ZOO VET CASEBOOK

The completed table should look like this:

WEEKS	0	1	2	3	4	5	6	7	8	9	10	11	12
Number of worms if the number of worms doubles every 3 weeks	1 WORM			2 WORMS			4			8			16
Every 2 weeks	1 WORM		2 WORMS		4		8		16 WORMS		32		64
Every week	1 WORM	2 WORMS	4	8	16	32	64	128	256	512	1024	2048	4096

CHALLENGE QUESTION

Answer: 21,000 worm eggs!

PAGES 16–17

ZOO VET CASEBOOK

1) The adult male gorilla is the heaviest (308 lb.).
2) The Goeldi monkeys are the lightest (12 oz.).
3) An adult male or female gibbon is heavier than an adult male ring-tailed lemur, but lighter than an adult female colobus monkey.
4) A golden lion tamarin (16 oz., or 1 lb.) and a crate (5.5 lb.) will weigh 6.5 lb.

CHALLENGE QUESTION

A spider monkey would balance the seesaw!

PAGES 18–19

ZOO VET CASEBOOK

1) 30 oz. 2) 2.5 oz. 3) 50 drops

CHALLENGE QUESTIONS

a) Grass: zebra and kangaroo
b) Bread: elephant and kangaroo
c) Chicken: Asiatic lion and wolf
d) Chocolate: Asiatic lion and wolf
e) Meat: elephant
f) Boxwood: zebra
g) Ragwort: kangaroo
h) Food bowl A (chicken): Asiatic lion and wolf
Food bowl B (vegetables): elephant and kangaroo
Food bowl C (straw): elephant and zebra

PAGES 20–21

ZOO VET CASEBOOK

1) The enclosure's **perimeter** is 920 feet.
2) 230 fence panels are needed.

CHALLENGE QUESTIONS

a) The space inside each enclosure is the same.
b) Enclosure D has the longest perimeter fence.

PAGES 22–23

ZOO VET CASEBOOK

1) 168 lb. 2) 4 weeks 3) 3 lb.
4) Because the bar lines go up the same amount each week (2 lb.).
5) 3 weeks

CHALLENGE QUESTION

Food can be placed at (1,1), (2,1), (2,2), (3,2)

PAGES 24–25

ZOO VET CASEBOOK

1) $15.94   2) 20¢   3) $6.05   4) 8 postcards
5) A pencil case and a set of three ballpoint pens ($6.50)
A gorilla and a zebra soft toy ($8.99)   6) $1.46

CHALLENGE QUESTIONS

a) 3 years ($4.50)   b) 1 year ($2.75)
c) A llama for 13 years ($19.50), a hippopotamus for 7 years ($19.25), or an elephant for 3 years ($15.75). (You could also adopt all three animals for 2 years.)

PAGES 26–27

ZOO VET CASEBOOK

1) The calf is fed at 6:00 a.m., 9:00 a.m., 12:00 p.m. (noon), 3:00 p.m., 6:00 p.m., 9:00 p.m.
2) 12 lb.   3) 2 lb.   4) 1 lb.   5) 1½ lb.

CHALLENGE QUESTIONS

a) • Baby A is a grey wolf   • Baby B is a lion
    • Baby C is a giant anteater   • Baby D is a gorilla
    • Baby E is a mountain zebra
b) Elephant, giraffe, mountain zebra, Malayan tapir, gorilla, lion, giant anteater, red river hog, grey wolf, panda, ring-tailed lemur, mouse

GLOSSARY

BREEDING PROGRAMS Zoos around the world work together to match up animals for breeding. If a species (type of animal) dies out in the wild, there will hopefully be a large and healthy population of that animal living in zoos. This will help to ensure that the species does not become extinct.

COLOSTRUM The first food produced by a mother to feed her baby. Colostrum is very nutritious (good for the baby) and contains antibodies, which kill germs and viruses.

CONSERVATION WORK Educating zoo visitors about wild animals, breeding endangered species, and taking part in research to understand how best to look after and protect wild animals.

ENDANGERED When a population of animals is growing smaller due to hunting or loss of habitat. Eventually the animals may become extinct.

GESTATION PERIOD The length of time that an animal or human is pregnant.

INSTINCTS Ways of acting that are natural to an animal. The animal has never been taught to act in this way but has inherited its response to particular situations from its ancestors.

PARASITIC When an organism (a living thing) lives in, or on, the body of another – for example, parasitic worms living in the stomachs of animals.

PRIMATES An animal group that includes monkeys, apes, and prosimians (animals such as lemurs). Humans are primates, too.

RESEARCH WORK Zoos study ways to give zoo animals an environment to live in that is as close as possible to their natural home. Zoos study feeding, disease, and reproduction. If zoo animals are happy and healthy, they are more likely to breed.

SEDATIVE A drug used to calm an animal or person. It can make the person or animal feel sleepy.

MATH GLOSSARY

AREA The measure of the size of a surface, made in squares (all of the same size).

DECIMAL FRACTIONS We use a counting system involving tens, multiples of ten, and fractions of ten. The decimal point separates whole numbers from decimal fractions. *For example, in the number 672.53, .53 stands for five tenths and three hundredths.*

FACES The flat surfaces of solid shapes.

FRACTIONS A fraction is a part of a whole. The bottom number of a fraction (denominator) tells how many parts the whole is divided into. The top number (numerator) tells how many parts of the whole you are referring to. If a shape is divided into four equal parts, each part is ¼ of the whole.

PERIMETER The distance all the way around a shape.

PRISM A solid shape the same size and shape all along its length. If you slice through a prism parallel to its end face, the cut faces will be the same size and shape as the ends. All the faces of a prism are flat (plane) and have three or more sides.

VERTICES These are corner points of flat (plane) shapes or 3-D shapes. For example, a cube has eight vertices.

t=top, b=bottom, c=center, l=left, r=right, OFC=outside front cover, OBC=outside back cover

Alamy: 8-9, 10, 12-13, 18-19, 27, OBC.
Corbis: 2-3, 17, 24-25, 29tl, 29tc. Paignton Zoo: 20-21, 22-23, 26.
Photodisc: OFC, 1, 6-7, 11, 14-15, 17. Ticktock Media: 16-17main, 29br.

Every effort has been made to trace the copyright holders, and we apologize in advance for any unintentional omissions. We would be pleased to insert the appropriate acknowledgements in any subsequent edition of this publication.